Play It!

LEVEL 1

A Superfast Way to Learn Awesome Songs on Your Guitar

CHILDREN'S SONGS FOR GUITAR

By Jennifer Kemmeter and Antimo Marrone

G
GRAPHIC ARTS
BOOKS®

Turner Publishing Company
Nashville, Tennessee
www.turnerpublishing.com

Library of Congress Control Number: 2025009786

ISBN: 9781513141961 (paperback) | 9781513141978 (hardbound) | 9781513141985 (e-book)

Published by Graphic Arts Books
an imprint of West Margin Press

WEST MARGIN PRESS
WestMarginPress.com

jenniferkemmeter.com

0 1 2 3 4 5 6 7 8 9

Contents

Hi Kids! My name is **Alan**. I'm going to teach you how to play music. Using my awesome system, you don't need to know anything fancy or technical—all you need is to know your colors, be able to follow a tune, and maybe even sing along. It's easy! Once you learn my cool, color-coded system, you'll be able to play a bunch of songs you probably already recognize, just by pressing the colors on the fretboard. Let's play!

Unsure what a song should sound like? Don't worry! We've collected all the songs in one place so you can listen to them!

Just scan this QR code, and any time you see this symbol:

find the corresponding letter or number and hit "download" to hear the song!

Introduction to the Guitar

Congratulations on your new guitar! We're going to have so much fun learning to play. Let's start by learning the parts of the guitar as shown in the diagram below.

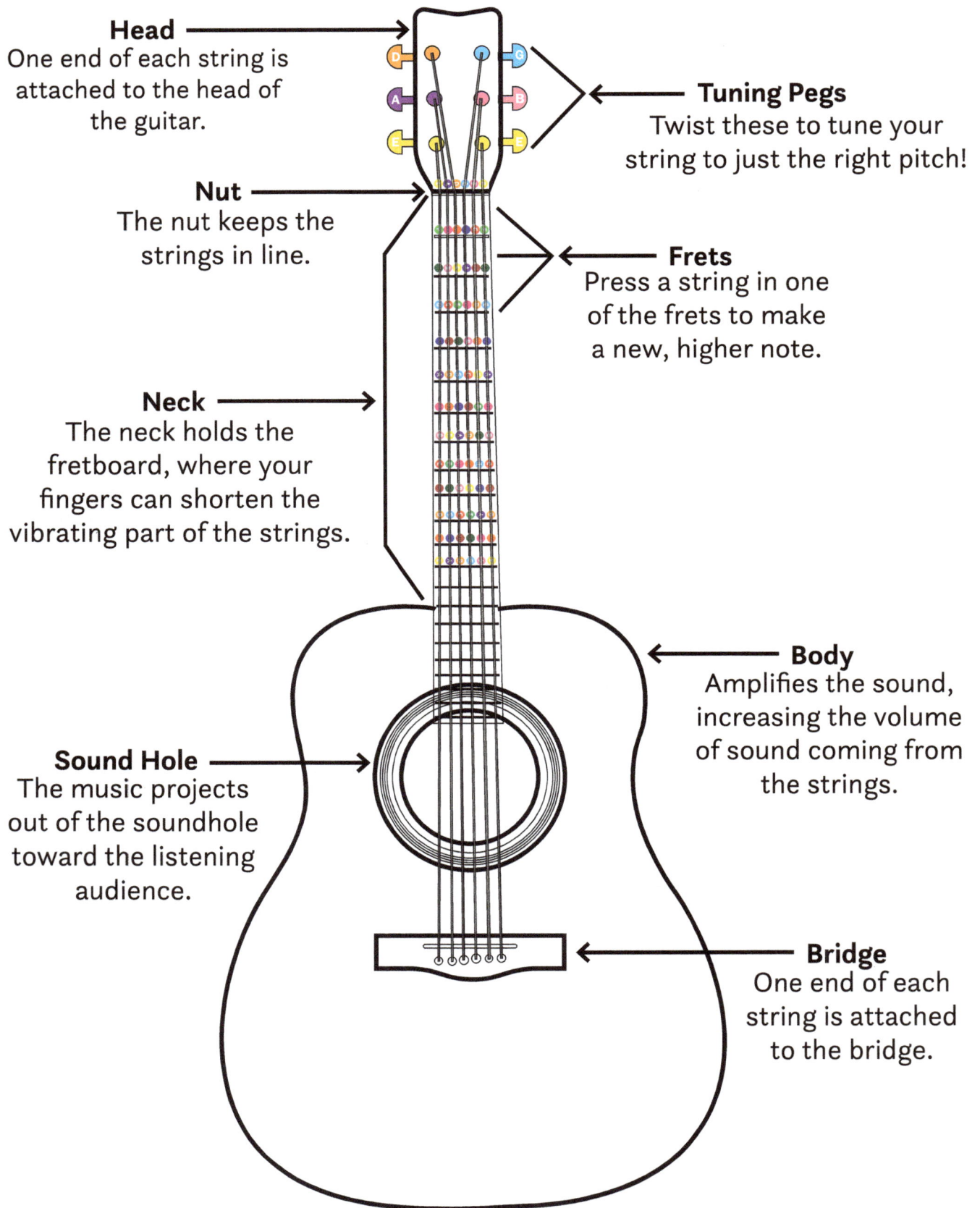

Head
One end of each string is attached to the head of the guitar.

Tuning Pegs
Twist these to tune your string to just the right pitch!

Nut
The nut keeps the strings in line.

Frets
Press a string in one of the frets to make a new, higher note.

Neck
The neck holds the fretboard, where your fingers can shorten the vibrating part of the strings.

Body
Amplifies the sound, increasing the volume of sound coming from the strings.

Sound Hole
The music projects out of the soundhole toward the listening audience.

Bridge
One end of each string is attached to the bridge.

Tuning the Strings

First things first! We start with the strings:

"Eddie Ate Dynamite, Good Bye Eddie"

There are 6 guitar strings, from **thickest at the top** to **thinnest at the bottom**. Each string is tuned to a note with a letter name.

The strings can be remembered with the acronym:

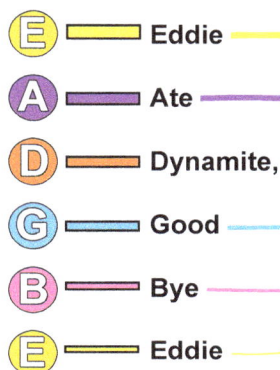

E — Eddie
A — Ate
D — Dynamite,
G — Good
B — Bye
E — Eddie

Tune your guitar with a digital headstock tuner before every session of play. This will make sure the strings sound the right notes. Start with the lowest pitch note on the thickest string, up to the highest, in the order **E-A-D-G-B-E**.

Many guitars come with a tuner and instructions, but if yours didn't, you can use our free tuner at jenniferkemmeter.com/guitar-childrens-audio.

The tuner clips on to the head of the guitar.

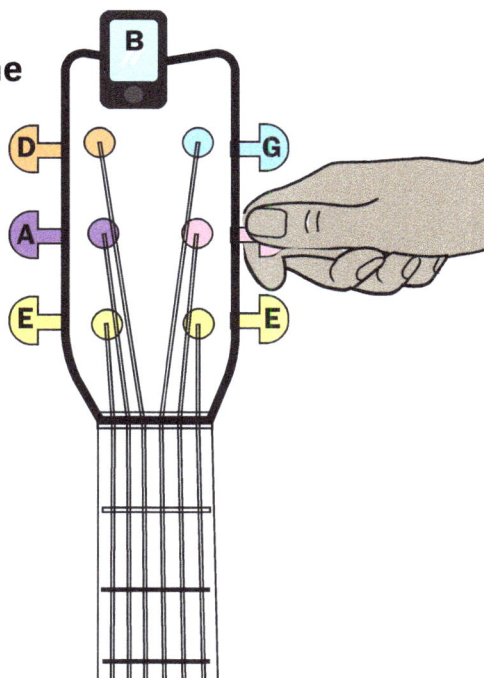

Color-Coding the Guitar

We color-code the notes in this book and on the guitar to make it easier to learn to play.

All you need to know are the rainbow colors to get started!

* Notes A B C D E F G are the natural notes, starting with the red C.
* A half-step up is called a sharp (#).
* A half-step down is called a flat (b).

C# C D E♭ E F F# G G# A B♭ B

Ow! That upward point is sharp!

Lie down flat to have a snooze.

Each string begins its own rainbow sequence of notes, starting with a different letter. Follow each string from left to right. Only the natural notes are labelled with a letter. **Press the string to the fretboard. This shortens the string to play a higher note.**

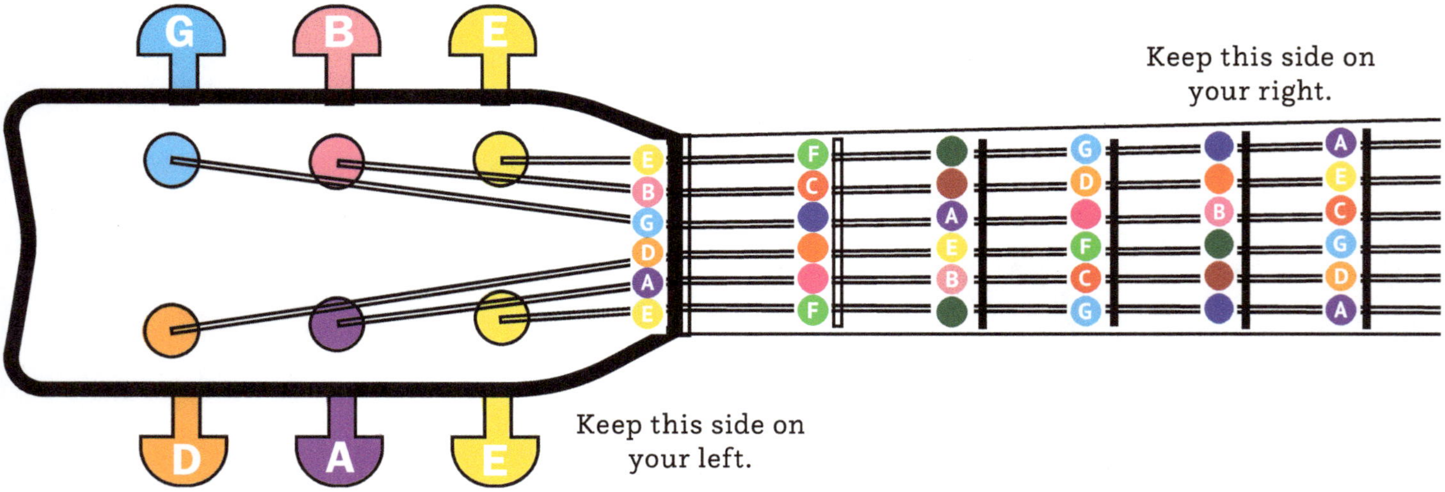

G   B   E

Keep this side on your right.

D   A   E

Keep this side on your left.

On page 57–61 of this book, you will find color labels for your guitar's fretboard. The labels go under the strings. They will help you match your fret fingering to the notes on the page.

Once you have set up your color-coded guitar, follow any string down the fretboard. Each fret down is a half-step note change, in the same order shown above.

Matching the TAB staff to the Guitar Strings

TAB is a staff of lines which tells you what string to play to sound a note.

When reading TAB, **imagine you've put the guitar face up on the table in front of you, with the head of the guitar on the left.** This aligns with the TAB staff as shown below.

The shape on a note tells you which finger to fret with.

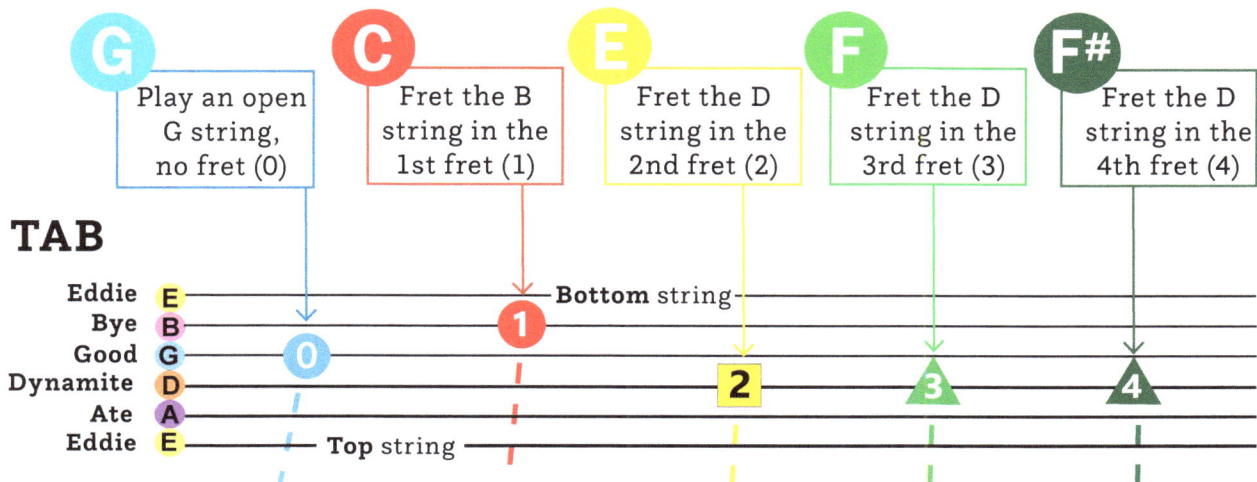

G — Play an open G string, no fret (0)

C — Fret the B string in the 1st fret (1)

E — Fret the D string in the 2nd fret (2)

F — Fret the D string in the 3rd fret (3)

F# — Fret the D string in the 4th fret (4)

TAB

Eddie — E — Bottom string
Bye — B — 1
Good — G — 0
Dynamite — D — 2   3   4
Ate — A
Eddie — E — Top string

GUITAR

Bottom string ... Top string

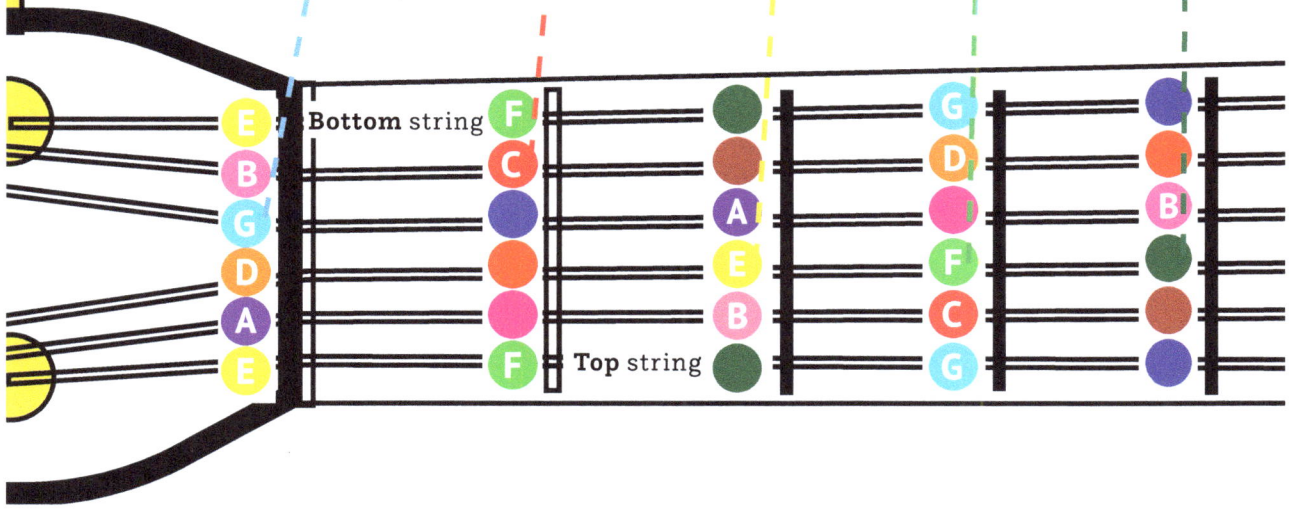

Putting it all together...

The TAB line the note is on tells you what string to play with the right hand, and fret with the left. The color tells you what note it is. The number tells you on what fret to press the string, and the shape tells you which finger to press with.

Pluck the string to play the note.

Preparing to Play

The way you hold your body, and hold the guitar, plays a big part in how good your music sounds. New players should sit with the guitar resting on the leg below their dominant hand.

To make sounds, we strum or pluck the strings over the soundhole. The six strings are all of different lengths and widths. If you push down on one of the strings at the frets as you play it, a higher note sounds out. The vibration of the strings resonates through the body of the guitar and the sound is projected out the sound hole.

Sound complicated? Don't worry! It's actually quite simple...

1. Place this book on a music stand so your posture is upright as you read the music. Adjust the stand so you play with your back straight and your head up. This way you can avoid back and neck strain, and see your music easily.

2. The dip of the guitar rests on the upper leg on the same side as your strumming hand. Right-handed players usually rest the guitar on their right leg, just below the chest.

3. The guitar front should be angled slightly upwards, to give you a view of the fret board.

4. The elbow of your fret hand should be at an angle smaller than 90 degrees. The smaller the angle, the less strain there will be on your wrist when it is reaching around the fretboard.

5. The elbow of your strumming arm should be at the top corner of the body of the guitar.

6. Cradle the upper part of the guitar neck between your thumb and the four fingers of your fret hand. The thumb rests lightly at the top of the neck or behind it.

Your left hand presses the strings to the fretboard...

...while your right hand plucks or strums the strings.

Left Hand on Fretboard

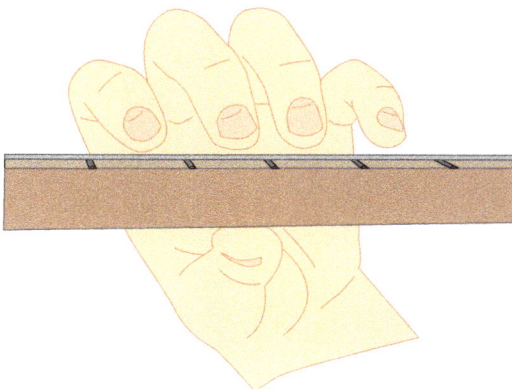

Right Hand over the Body

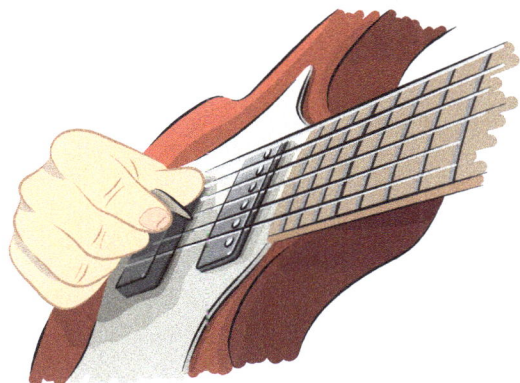

Playing Notes

Let's start by playing different notes on the same string.

Play the first string open, then press the string down in the 1st fret and play the same string. Step down the fretboard with the next finger on each next fret. Each note in TAB shows you which finger of your left hand to use to fret the note. The hand diagram below the TAB staff shows what string to play and where to fret. The number is the fret in which you press the string.

The high E string.

0   **1**   **2** — **Bottom** string — **3**

"2" = 2nd fret

Top string

E   F   F#   G

The B string.   The G string.

0   **1**   **2**   **3**   **0**   **1**   **2**   **3**   **Bottom** string –

Top string

B   C   C#   D   G   G#

The D string.   The A string.   The low E string.

0   **1**   **2**   **3**   **0**   **1**   **2**   **3**   **0**   **1**   **2**   **3**

D   D#   E   F   A   Bb   B   C   E   F   F#   G

NOTE: **0** **0** **0** **0** and **0** are all open notes, where no strings are pressed at a fret.

The bottom 3 lines of the TAB staff are darkened to show the heavier, copper-wound strings.

Note Timing and Note Length

4 The Time Signature, Notes, and Measures

The Time Signature tells us how to count time. The top number tells us how many beats are in a measure. The note below it tells you what kind of note gets one beat. This time signature tells us there are 4 beats in a measure, and a quarter note gets one best.

The TAB staff is divided by vertical lines. The space between a pair of vertical lines is called a measure. This is a unit of time, made up of a number of beats, shown in the top number of the time signature.

 # beats per measure.

1 measure

Ma – ry   had   a   lit – tle lamb,   lit – tle lamb,   lit – tle lamb.

Note which gets 1 beat.

Below the staff are the **Note Stems**. The stems tells you how long to hold the note for (see below).

Note stems tell you how long to hold the note

Time duration of note stems:

An **Eighth Note** is held for **1/2 beat**.	A **Quarter Note** is held for **1 beat**.	A **Dotted Quarter Note** is held for **1.5 beats**.	A **Half Note** is held for **2 beats**.	A **Dotted Half Note** is held for **3 beats**.	A **Whole Note** is held for **4 beats**.

To stop the string or strings from vibrating, roll your strumming hand to the right so the side of your palm pushes lightly on all the strings at once, over the soundhole. This will mute the strings.

Don't worry if you don't get all this at first! It will take a few practice sessions to feel comfortable with your new instrument.

Strumming Chords

Guitarists play notes (one string at a time), and strum chords (many strings together). **Learn to play the notes of the songs in this book first, then go through the book again and learn to strum the chords.**

To play a chord, first set your fingers to the fretboard. These are some chords you will find in this book:

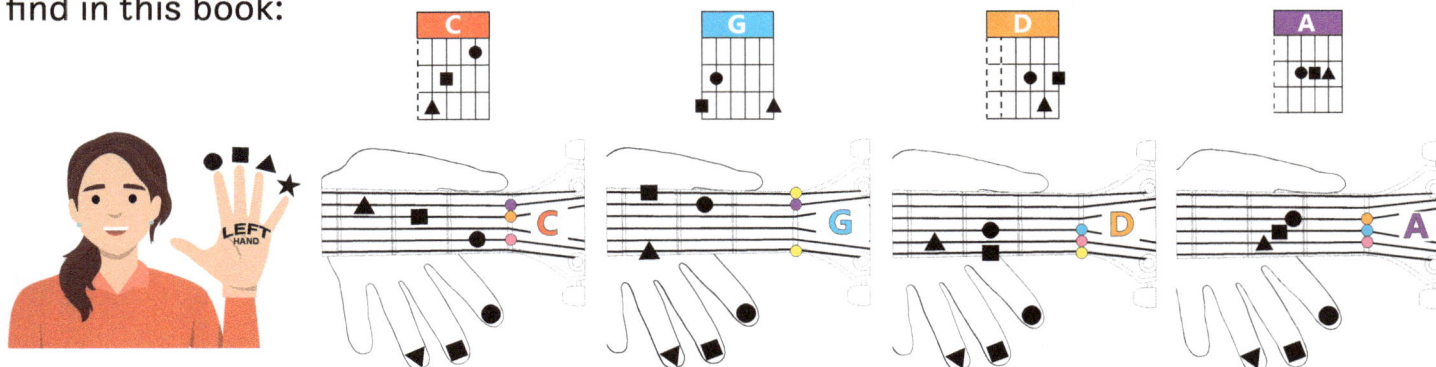

The **black shapes** tell you which fingers, on which strings, and in which fret.

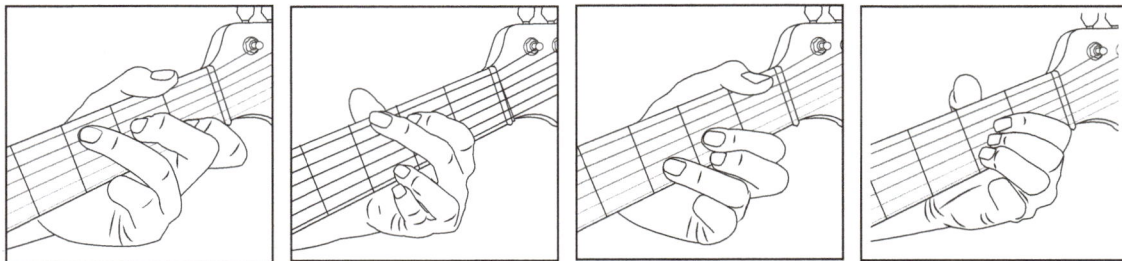

Reading a Chord Chart

A sample chord chart is shown below.

The chord chart is a vertical version of the guitar's upper fretboard. Imagine turning the chord chart clockwise 90 degrees as below. This shows you the frets to play and which fingers to use.

C Chord

C

1st Fret →
2nd Fret →
3rd Fret →

Strings

Top String

Bottom String

Strum only the solid line strings!

C

Strumming Patterns and Time

Strumming is playing many strings together in downstrokes and upstrokes with the right hand. You should use a guitar pick to get the right sound.

Always clap out the strumming pattern first.

This will help you avoid an awkward tangle-up!

Read: **"One..... Two-and, Three..., Four-and"**

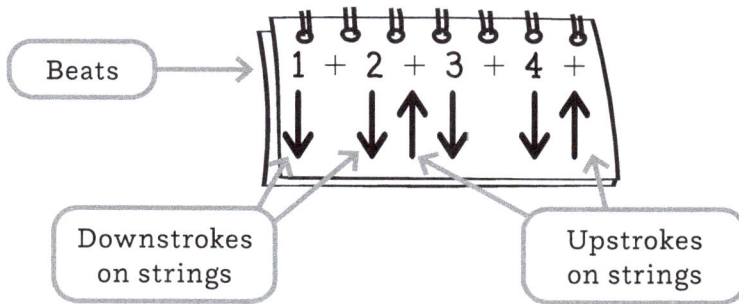

Clap out the strumming patterns below. When you encounter a new pattern, clap it out first and practice it repeatedly until it feels relaxed and easy.

3

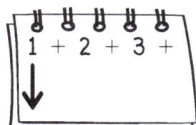

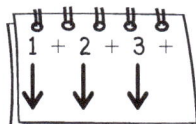

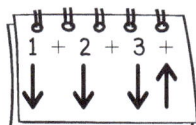

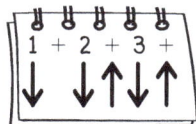

4

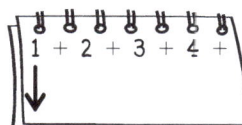

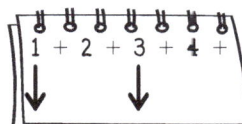

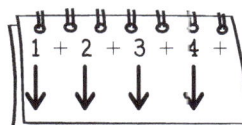

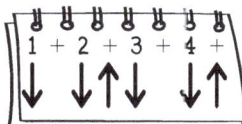

This is the **bottom** string

("3" = 3rd Fret)

This is the **top** string

3rd Fret

1st Fret

3rd Fret

2nd Fret

G

C

D

A

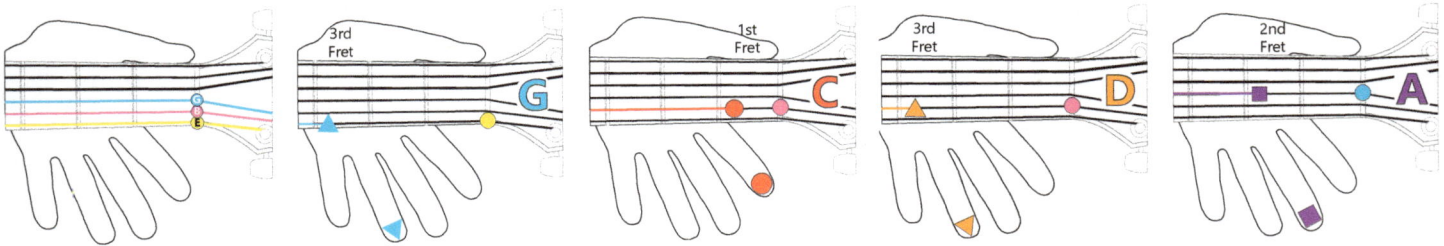

1. Mary Had a Little Lamb

C   G   C

Ma – ry   had   a   lit – tle   lamb,   lit – tle   lamb,   lit – tle   lamb.

G   C

Ma – ry   had   a   lit – tle   lamb,   it's   fleece   was   white   as   snow.

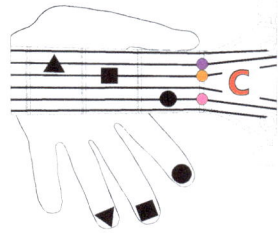

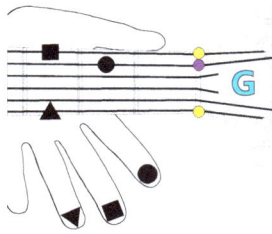

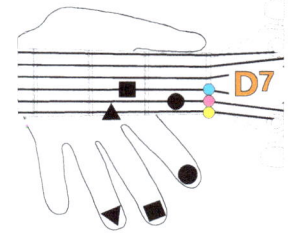

2. Row, Row, Row Your Boat

Row, row, row your boat, gent – ly down the stream.
Row, row, row your boat, gent – ly down the stream.

Mer–ri–ly, mer–ri–ly, mer–ri–ly merrily, life is but a dream!
If you see a croc–o–dile, don't for – get to scream!

Repeat
1 time

E — O — Bottom string

B — O —

G — O — T A B

D — — 2 —

A —

E — Top string —

G   D

3. Hot Cross Buns 🔊 3

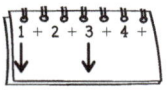

1 + 2 + 3 + 4 +

G

E						
B	4	0			0	
G			2	0		2	0

Hot   cross   buns,   Hot   cross   buns,

D   G

E												
B									0		
G	0	0	0	0	2	2	2	2		2	0

One a pen – ny, two a pen – ny, Hot cross buns.

Two Eighth Notes are each held for **1/2 beat.**

4. Skip to My Lou

Skip, skip,   skip to my Lou,   Skip, skip,   skip to my Lou!

Skip, skip,   skip to my Lou,   Skip to my Lou my   dar - lin'.

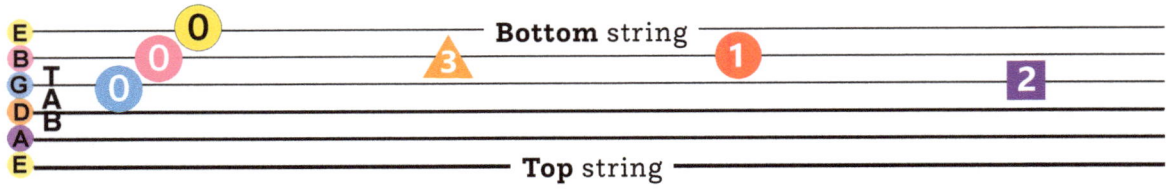

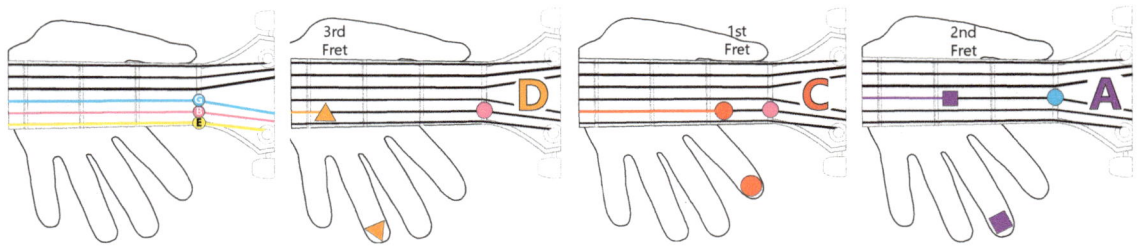

5. This Old Man

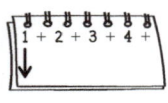

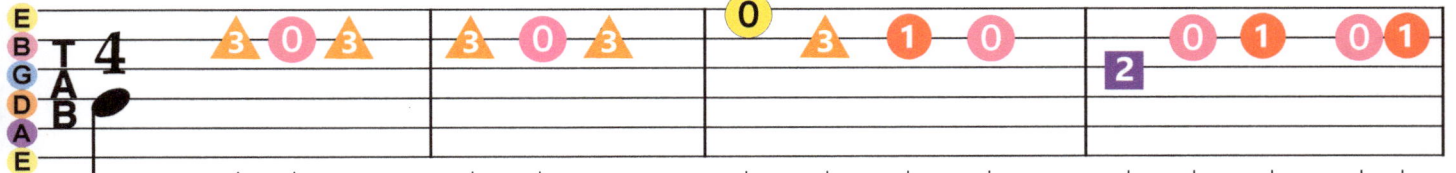

This old man,   he played one,   he played knick-knack   on my thumb, with a

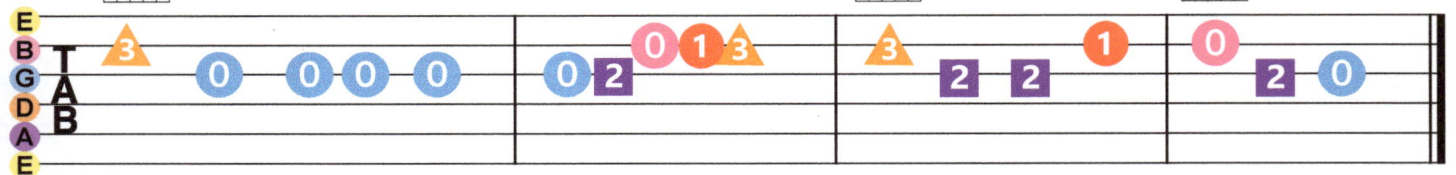

knick knack, pad-dy whack,   give a dog a bone.   This old man came   roll-ing home.

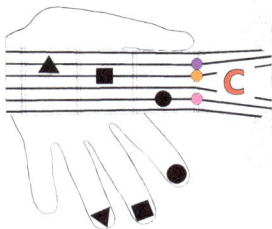
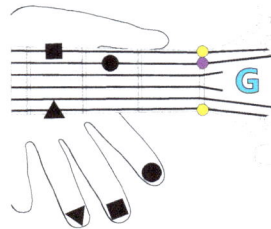
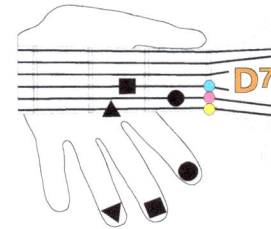
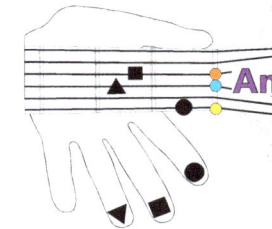

6. Kum ba yah

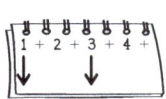

Kum ba   yah, my Lord,   Kum ba yah.   Kum ba yah, my   Lord, Kum ba

yah. Kum ba   yah, my Lord,   Kum ba yah.   Oh Lo-rd, Kum ba yah.

Tip Break!
Top Tips for Playing Notes

1. Practice playing the notes in the song first.

Look at the notes in the diagrams above the song, and practice playing those notes, and moving between those notes. This will get you warmed up to play the new tune.

2. Clap out the rhythm of the song before you play it.

You probably know a lot of the songs in this book already, but for any you don't know, clap through the song using the note-stem line, so you know how long to hold each note for.

3. Learn to play each song in sections.

You won't be able to look at the music, and the guitar, at the same time. It's easier if you learn to play a few notes at a time, practice the series and memorize how to play the phrase, then move on to the next section.

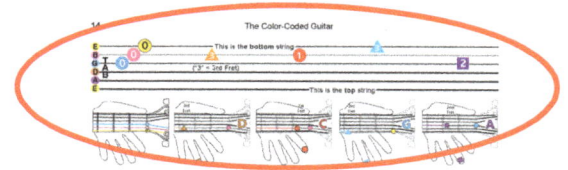

Tip Break!
Top Tips for Fretting

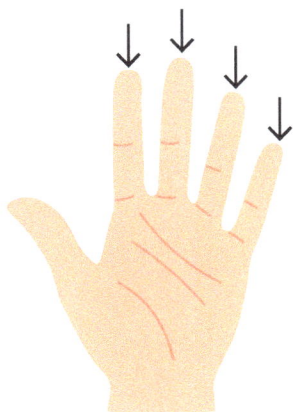

1. Fret with the tip of the finger, not the side or pad.

The strings are close together. Press the strings with the top of your finger, so you don't accidentally press other strings. Your hand and fingers will curl around the fretboard in a C shape.

2. Press the string near the metal fret.

This will create the best sound on your strings when you pluck or strum, you won't have to push as hard on the string, and it will minimize finger pain as you get started with guitar.

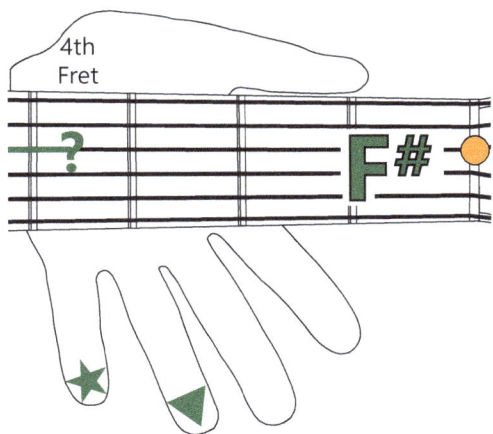

3. Use the finger that works best for you.

Some people prefer to use the ring finger in the fourth fret, some prefer the pinky. It depends how much your hand can stretch, how strong your fingers are, and when you feel comfortable moving your whole hand up and down the fretboard. Your fingers will get stronger the more you play and your hands grow, so you may change how you fret notes over time.

24

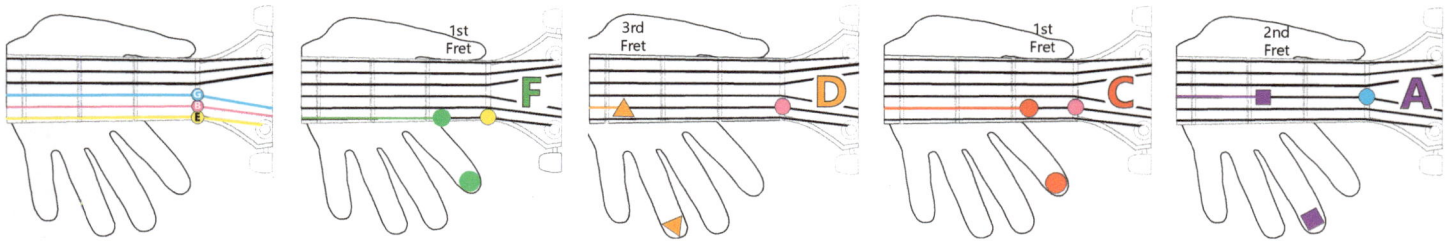

7. Home on the Range

25

8. Bingo

There was a farm-er had a dog and Bin-go was his

name - o! B I N G O! B I

N G O! B I N G O! and Bin-go was his name - o!

9. London Bridge

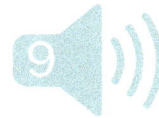

G		**D7**	**G**

Lon – don bridge is   fall – ing down,   fall – ing down,   fall – ing down.
Build   it   up with   wood and clay,   wood and clay,   wood and clay.

	D7	**G**

Lon – don Bridge   is   fall – ing down,   My   fair,   la – dy.
Build   it   up with   wood and clay,   My   fair   la – dy.

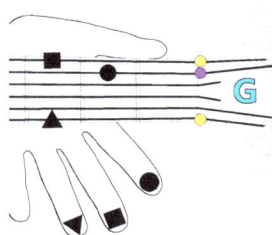

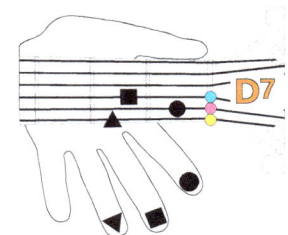

10. Three Blind Mice

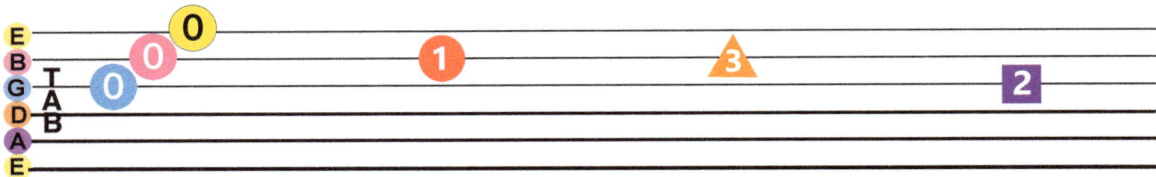

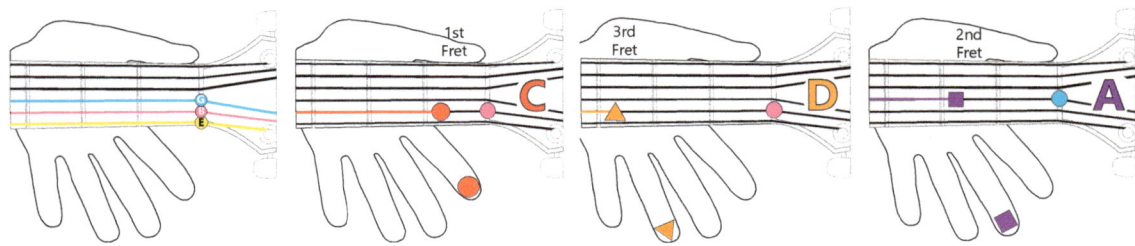

11. Twinkle, Twinkle Little Star

Twin-kle, twin-kle lit - tle star, how I wond-er what you are!

Up a - bove the world so high, like a dia-mond in the sky.

Twin-kle, twin-kle lit - tle star, how I wond-er what you are!

C   G   D7

♩ = 1 beat

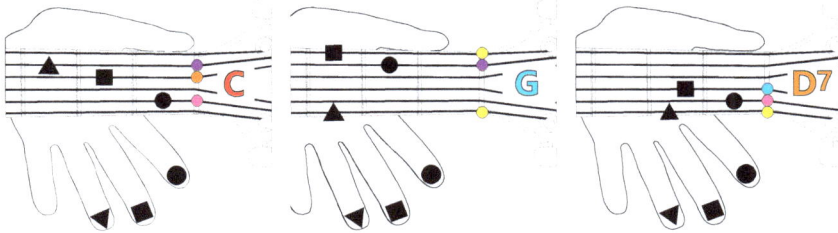

12. When the Saints Go Marching In

12

G

Oh when the saints go march-ing in, oh when the saints go
Oh when the sun be-gins to shine, oh when the sun be –

D7   G   C

march-ing in. Then let me be a – mong that num-ber
gins to shine. Oh how I want to be in that num-ber

G

oh when the saints go march – ing in.
oh when the sun be – gins to shine.

Repeat 1 time

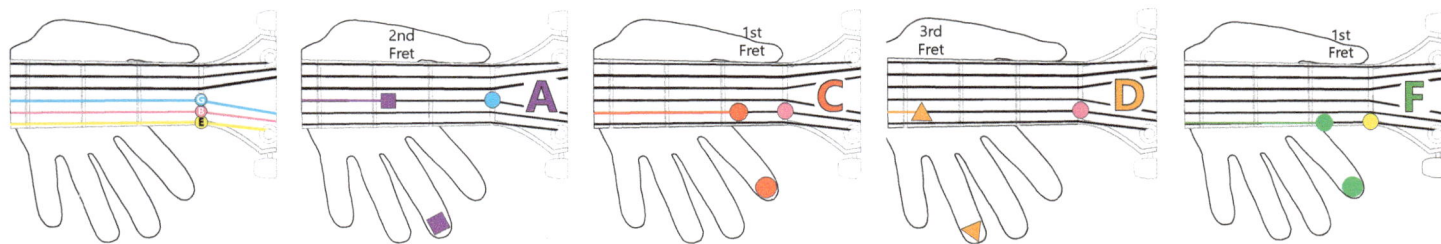

13. Baa Baa Black Sheep

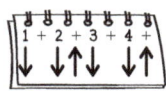

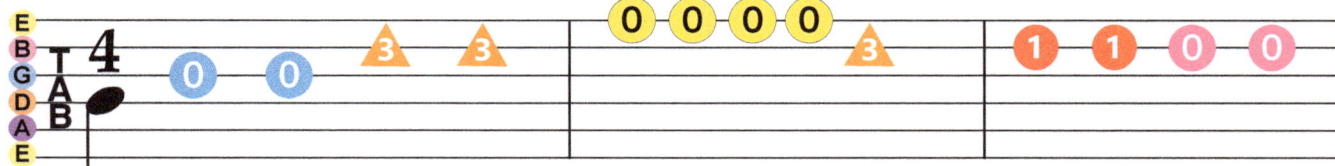

Baa, baa black sheep, have you a – ny wool? Yes sir, yes sir,

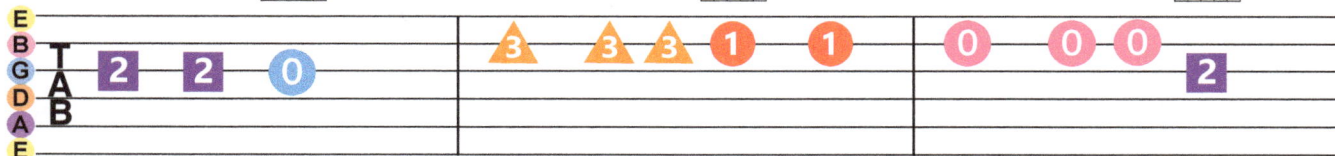

three bags full. One for my mas – ter, one for the dame,

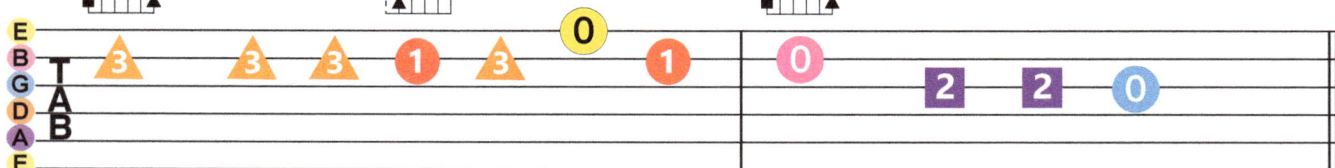

one for the lit – tle boy who lives down the lane.

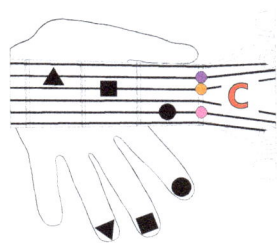

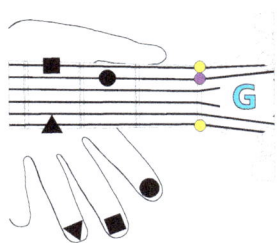

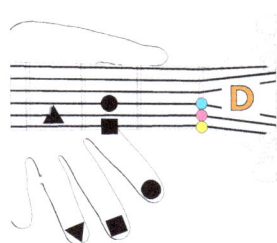

14. Happy Birthday

C   G   D

Hap – py   birth–day   to   you,   Hap–py   birth–day   to   you,   Hap–py

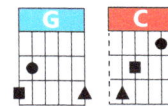

birth – day   dear   [name   here],   Hap–py   birth – day   to   you!

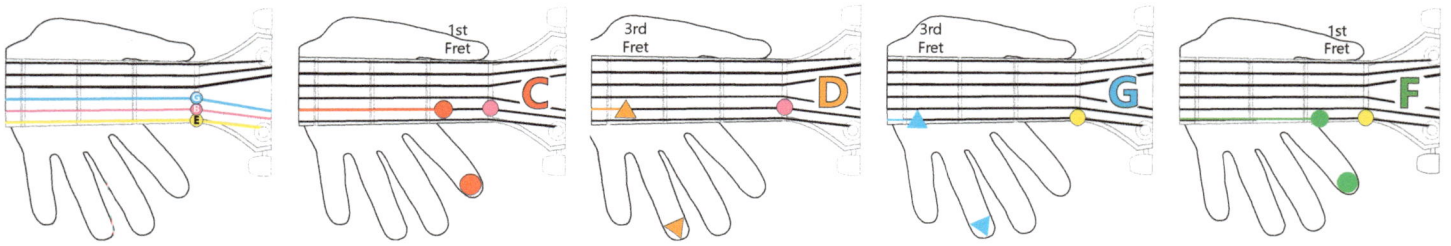

15. The Wheels on the Bus

15 🔊

The wheels on the bus go round and round, round and round,
The wipers on the bus go swish, swish, swish, swish, swish, swish,

round and round. The wheels on the bus go round and round, all through town.
swish, swish, swish. The wipers on the bus go swish, swish, swish, all through town.

Repeat
1 time

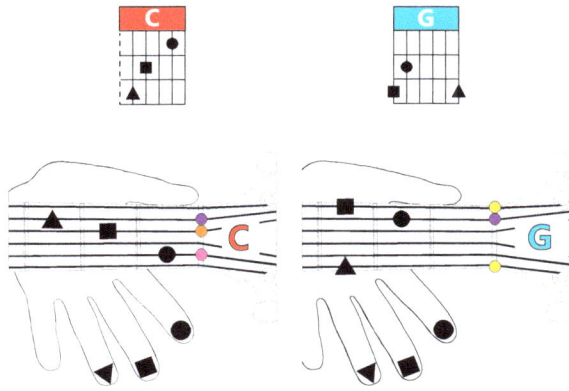

16. Ode to Joy

Joy – ful, joy–ful, we a–dore Thee, God of glo–ry, Lord of love. Hearts un–fold like

flow'rs be – fore Thee, op'–ning to the sun a–bove. Melt the clouds of sin a–nd sad–ness;

Drive th–e dark of doubt a–way! Giv–er of im – mor–tal glad–ness, fill us with the light of day!

17. Are You Sleeping?

Are you sleep-ing?   Are you sleep-ing?   Broth-er John,   Broth-er John!

Morn-ing bells are ring-ing!   Morn-ing bells are ring-ing!   Ding, dang, dong.   Ding, dang, dong.

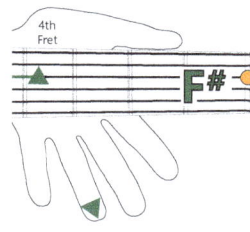

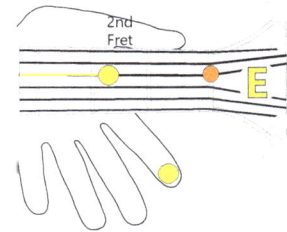

18. The Muffin Man

Do you know the muf – fin man, the muf – fin

man, the muf – fin man? Do you know the

muf – fin man who lives on Drur – y Lane?

36

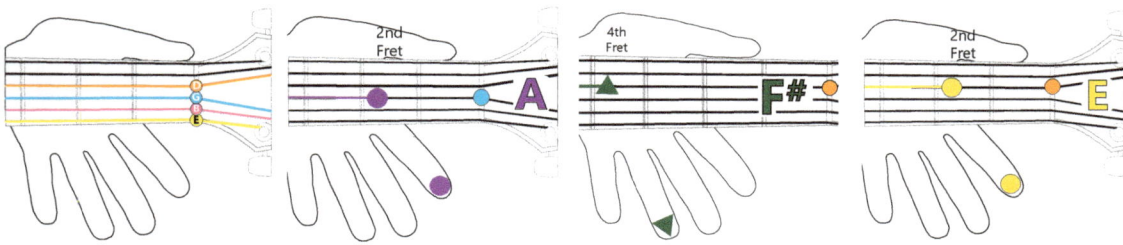

19. Alphabet Song

19

A B C D E F G H I J K L M N O P

Q R S T U V Double-U X Y and Z.

Now I know my A B C's, next time won't you sing with me?

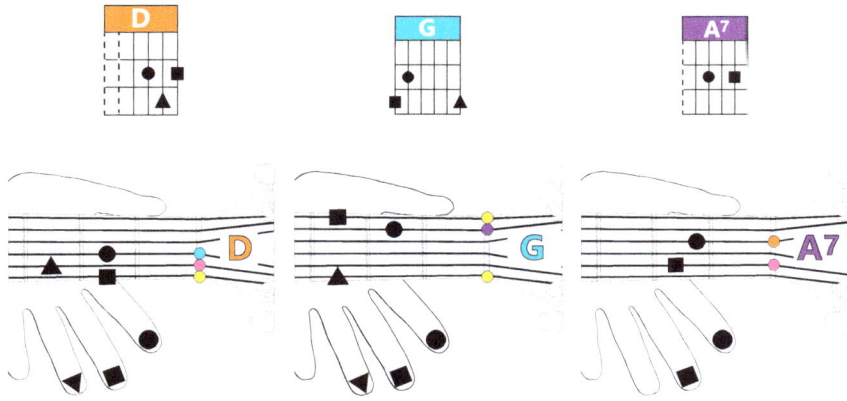

20. Hickory Dickory Dock

Hick - o - ry, dick - o - ry dock. ——— The mouse— ran

up — the clock. ——— The clock struck one, the

mouse ran down, hick - o - ry dick - o - ry dock!

Tip Break!

Top Tips for Strumming Chords

1. Practice chord changes.

Finger placement on the frets when changing chords can really slow down play. Practice playing each of the chords of your song first, with special attention to making quick chord changes.

Exercise: 1-minute changes

Choose 2 chords (we recommend starting with C and G). Set a stopwatch for 1 minute. See how many times you can strum each chord, by switching back and forth for one minute. Work up to 30, and aim for 60!

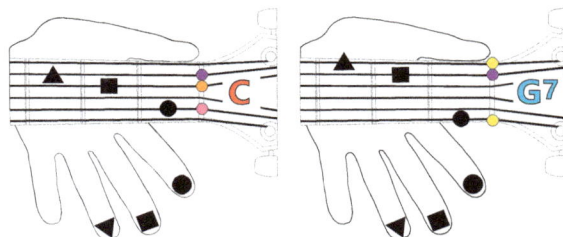

2. Practice the strumming pattern many, many times first.

- First clap out the strumming pattern 10 times.
- Second, silent-strum the pattern on your guitar 10 times. You can mute the strings by resting the side of your strumming palm on the strings while you strum.
- Thirdly, unmute the strings and strum each chord in your song with that pattern.
- Finally, play the song.

3. Learn to play each song in sections.

The same concept from playing notes applies here—you won't be able to look at the music, and the guitar, at the same time. Learn to play a few meaasures at a time, memorize the chord changes, then move on to the next section.

Tip Break!
Top Tips for Controlling Note or Chord Duration

1. Keep good time.

Gently bounce your left heel against the floor with the time signature as you play. This will help you keep time with the song and track note duration.

2. Use the side of your right hand palm to mute strings when needed.

Play notes and chords with the side of your right palm just above the strings. After plucking or strumming you can quickly mute the strings by pressing your side-palm to all strings.

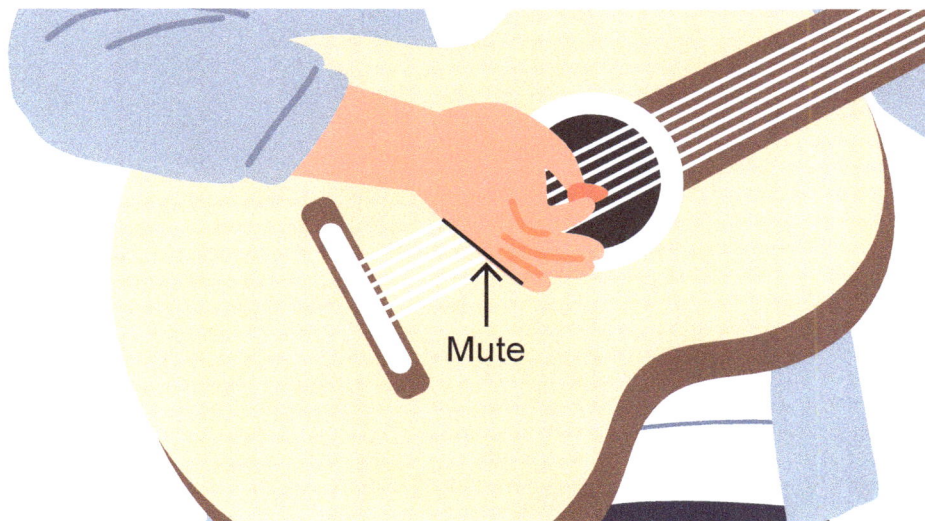

Mute

3. When playing a fast tempo, keep the strumming or plucking motion small.

One of the challenges of playing guitar is making changes with your hands quickly, to keep up with the music. Keep motions small, strong and close to the instrument for faster play.

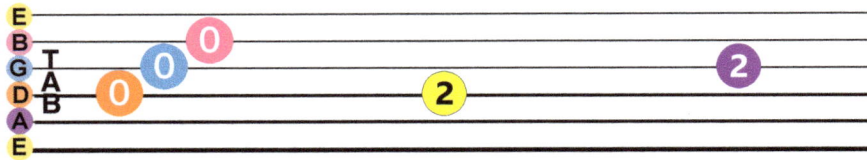

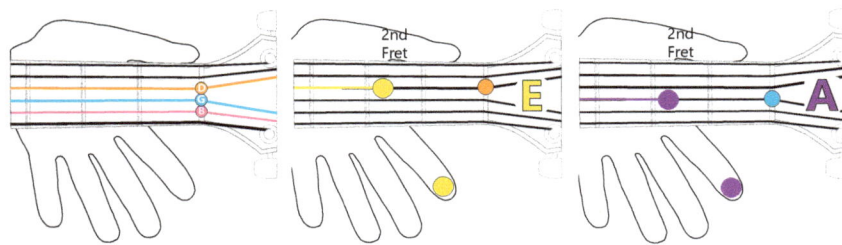

21. Old MacDonald

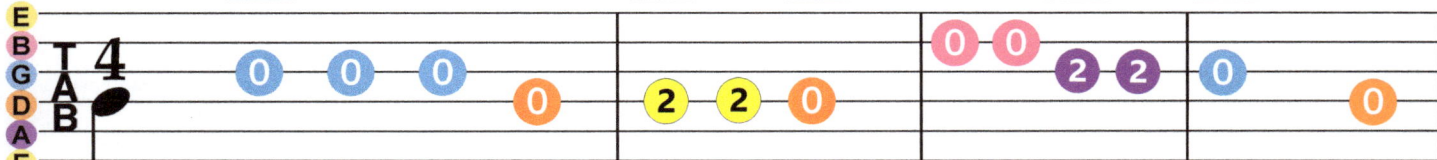

Old Mac – Don – ald had a farm, E – I – E – I – O! And
on his farm he had some chick-ens, E – I – E – I – O! With a

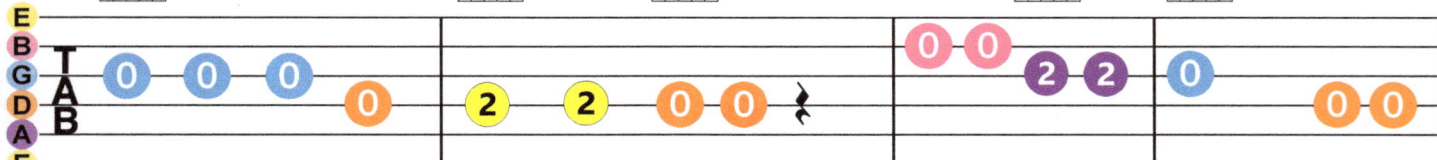

Keep the song going! Try out some more animals like our farm friends here and imitate their sounds!

cluck   cluck   here!   And   a   cluck   cluck   there!   Here   a   cluck!   There   a   cluck!

Eve–ry–where a cluck cluck!   Old Mac–Don–ald   had   a   farm,   E – I – E – I – O!

22. Clementine

In a ca-vern, in a can-yon, ex-ca-va-ting for a mine dwelt a

mi – ner, for-ty – ni – ner and his daugh – ter, Cle-men – tine. Oh my

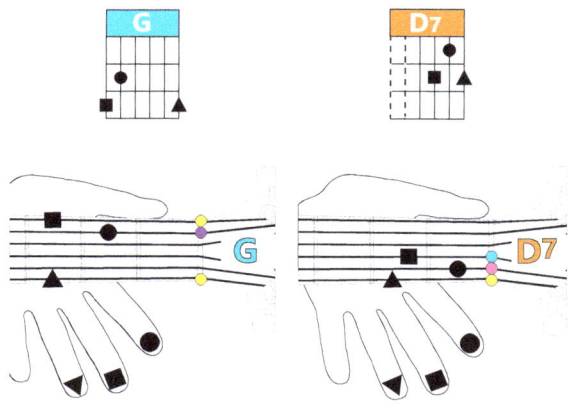

dar – ling,   oh my   dar – ling,   oh my   dar – ling Cle-men – tine,   you are

lost   and   gone for – ev – er.   Dread-ful   sor – ry,   Cle-men – tine.

23. Pop! Goes the Weasel

'Round   and   round   the   cob – bl – er's   bench,   Mon – key

chased   the   wea – sel.   Mon – key   thought   'twas

all   in   good   fun.   Pop!   goes   the   wea – sel.

Tip Break!
Top Tips for Improving Left Hand Dexterity and Speed

1. Do Spider Exercises.

Turn to page 12. Set each finger to a fret, and play notes up and down a string, walking with your fingers, one fret at a time. Play through 4 frets on each string, up and down the fretboard.

2. Loosen Up the Wrist.

Keep your left hand loose and active, especially as you reach for the low E and A strings at the top of the fretboard. Be ready to rotate the hand for a wider C, and move the hand back and forth along the fretboard as needed.

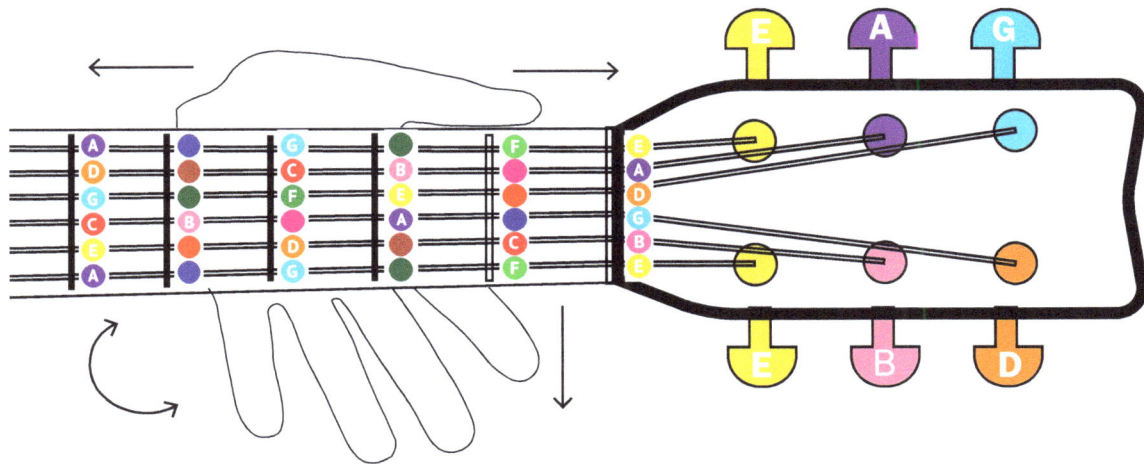

3. Try Rolling to a Finger Pad.

When you have to play two adjacent strings in the same fret in sequence, roll the pad of your fretting finger between the two. Practice a few times before playing the song. Here's an example from "Three Blind Mice":

farm–er's wife, who   cut off their tails with a   carv – ing knife, did you

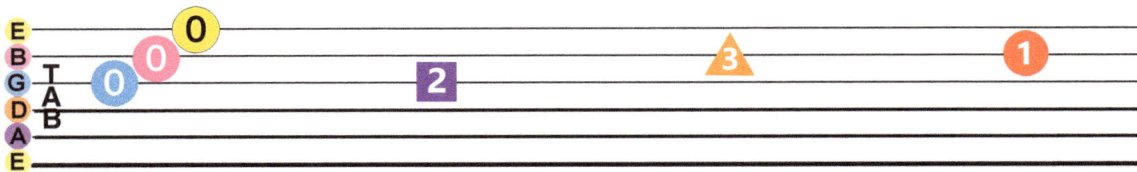

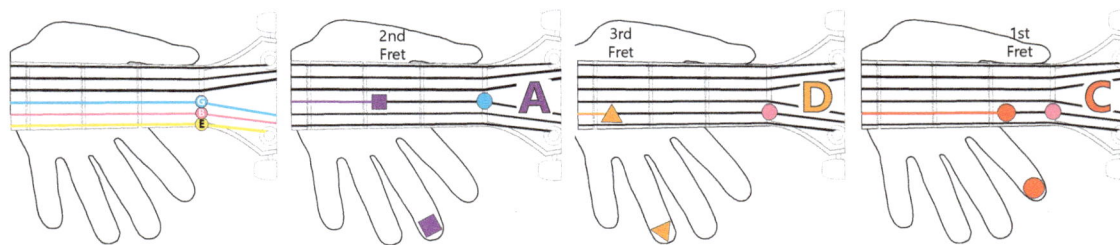

46

24. Oh! Susanna

For I come from Al - a - bam-a with a ban-jo on my knee For I'm

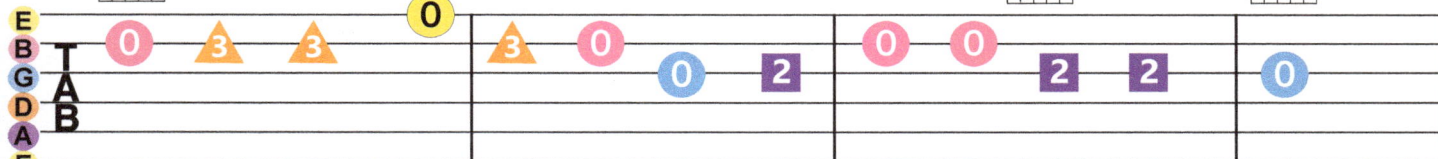

goin' to Loui - si - an - a my —— true love for to see.

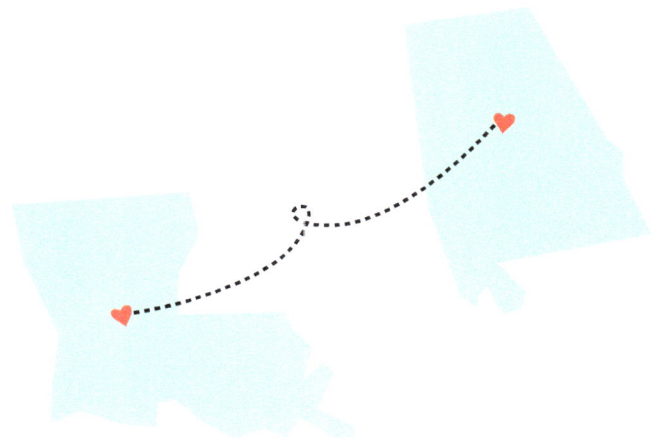

Oh! Su – sann – a, oh don't you cry for me; For I

come from Al – a – bam – a with a ban – jo on my knee.

25. Drunken Sailor

25 🔊

Em | **D**

| What | shall | we | do | with | a | drunk-en | sail – or? | What | shall | we | do | with | a |

Em | **G**

| drunk-en sail-or? | What | shall | we | do | with | a | drunk-en | sail – or? | Earl-y | in | the |

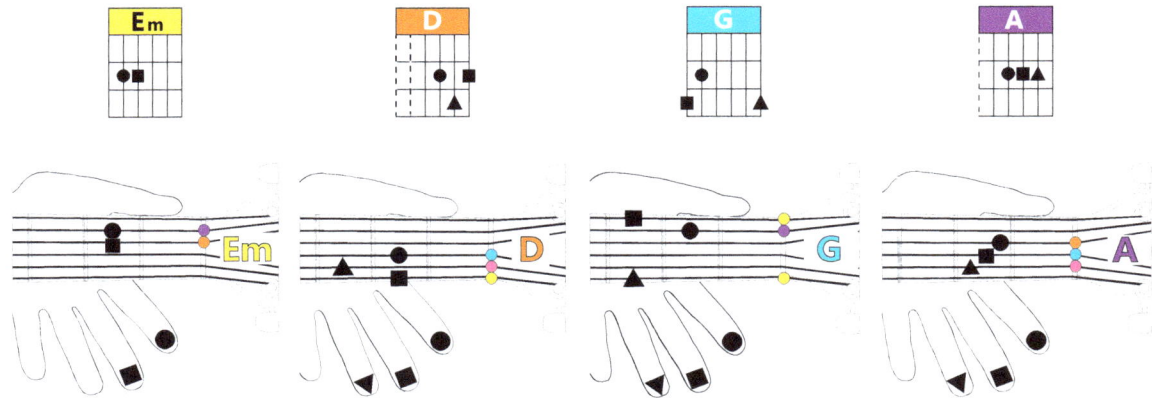

26. Scarborough Fair

Are you going to Scar – bor-ough Fair?

Pars – ley, sage, rose – mar – y and thyme.

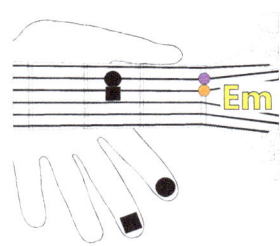
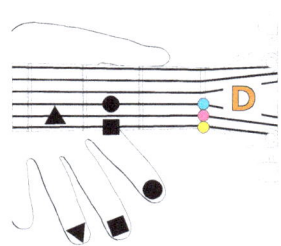
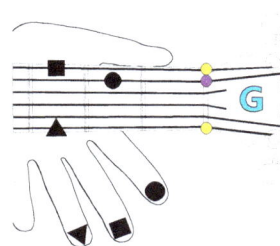
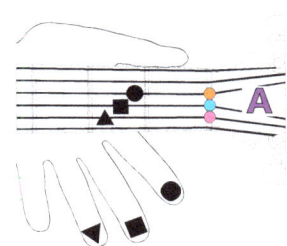

Re – mem – ber me to one who lives there.

For once she was a true love of mine.

= 2 beats

= 4 beats

27. My Bonnie Lies Over the Ocean

My Bon-nie lies o-ver the o-cean.— My Bon-nie lies o-ver the sea.— My

Bon-nie lies o-ver the o-cean.— Oh, bring back my Bon-nie to me.— Bring

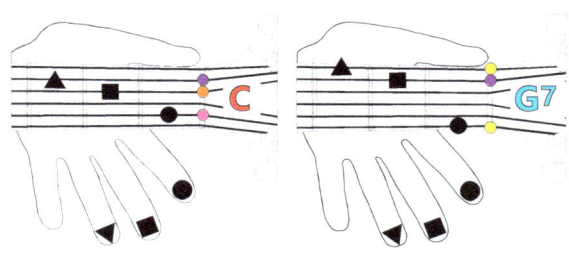

back, bring back, oh bring back my Bon-nie to me, to me! Bring

back, bring back, oh bring back my Bon-nie to me!

28. Clock Chimes

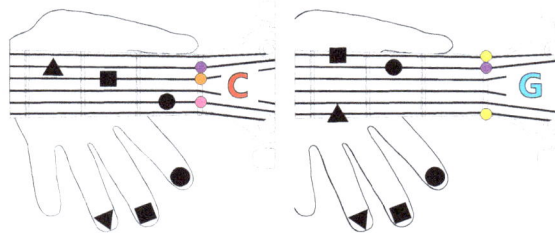

29. Ring Around the Rosie

Ring a-round the ro – sie, a pock – et – full of pos – ies.

Ash – es, ash – es, we all fall down.

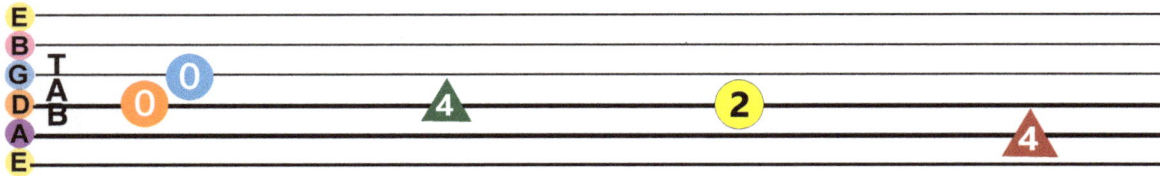

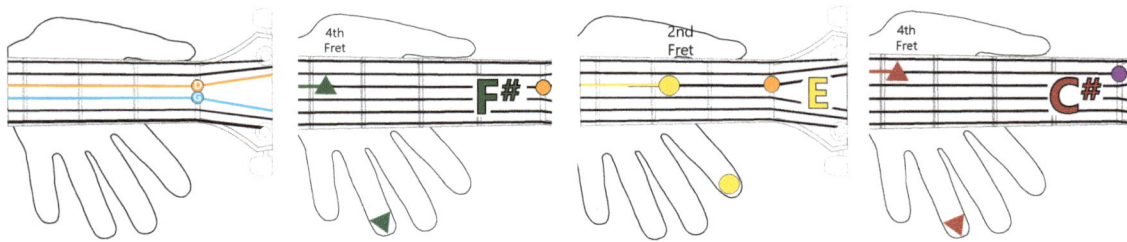

30. The Grand Old Duke of York

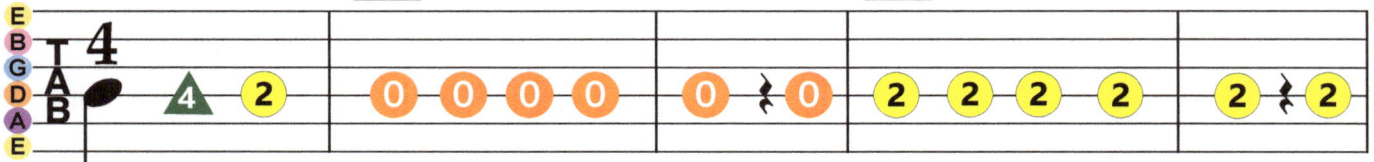

D   **A⁷**

Oh, the   grand old Duke of   York,   he   had   ten thous–and   men. He

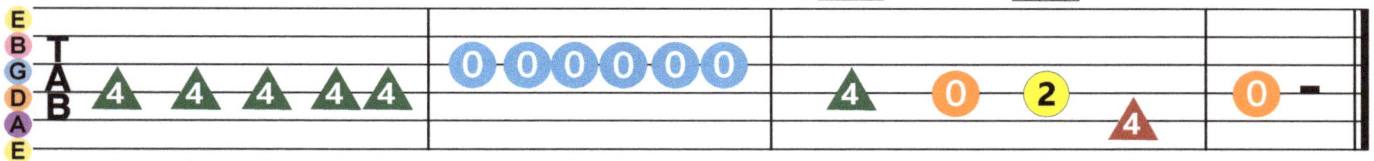

D   **G**   **D**   **A⁷**   **D**

marched them up to the   top of the hill and he   marched them down   a – gain.

Fretboard Labels

You will need scissors and scotch tape!

Instructions

1. Choose a set of labels on the next page or page 61 which matches your guitar size, and cut along the white lines. You will only play notes in the first 4 frets in this book, so you can tape just those onto your guitar if you prefer. We include labels for 12 frets.

2. Run label strips beneath strings in the fret which matches the number at the bottom of the strip. Each dot should be beneath a string. See diagram below. Put the string label (0) to the left of the nut, and the 1st fret label just left of the 1st fret.

3. Fold the strip over the neck, and tape each end to the back of the guitar neck to hold the label strip in place. The label should be flat and tight to the fretboard, so tape it tightly! (A loose label may interfere with the vibration of the guitar strings.)

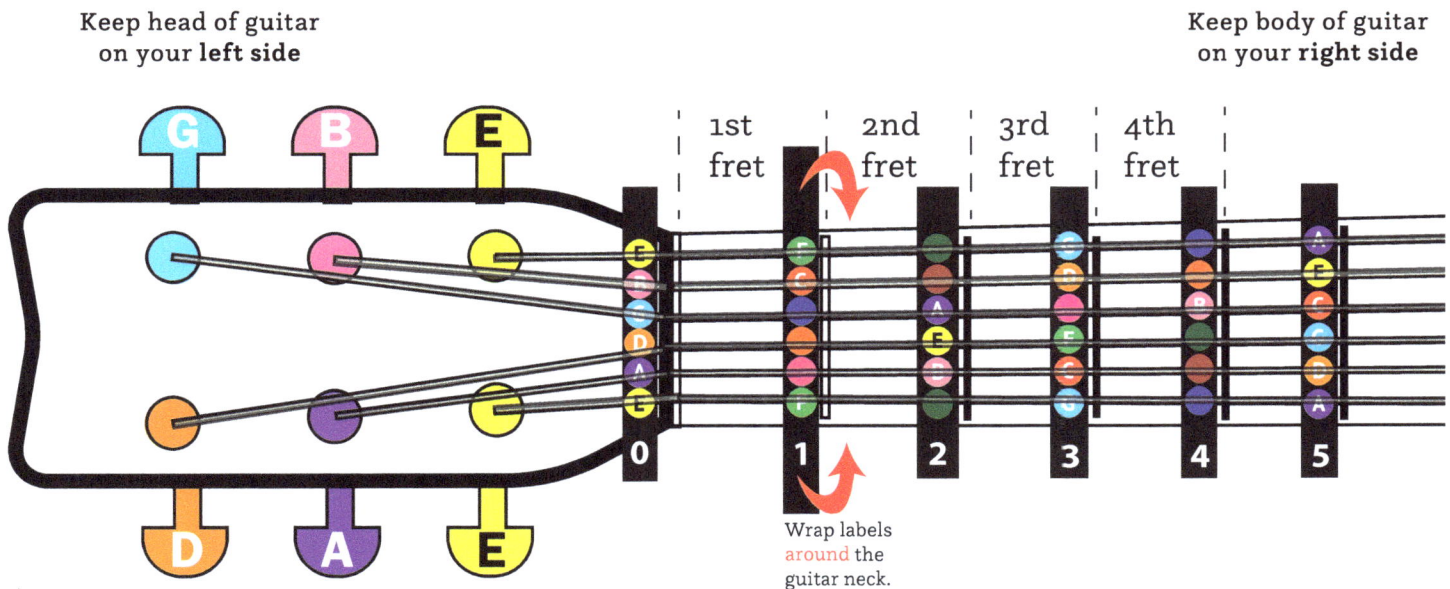

Keep head of guitar on your **left side**

Keep body of guitar on your **right side**

Wrap labels around the guitar neck.

Full Size Electric Guitar (Age 12+)
Full Size Narrow-Neck Acoustic
1/2 Size Acoustic (Age 5–8)

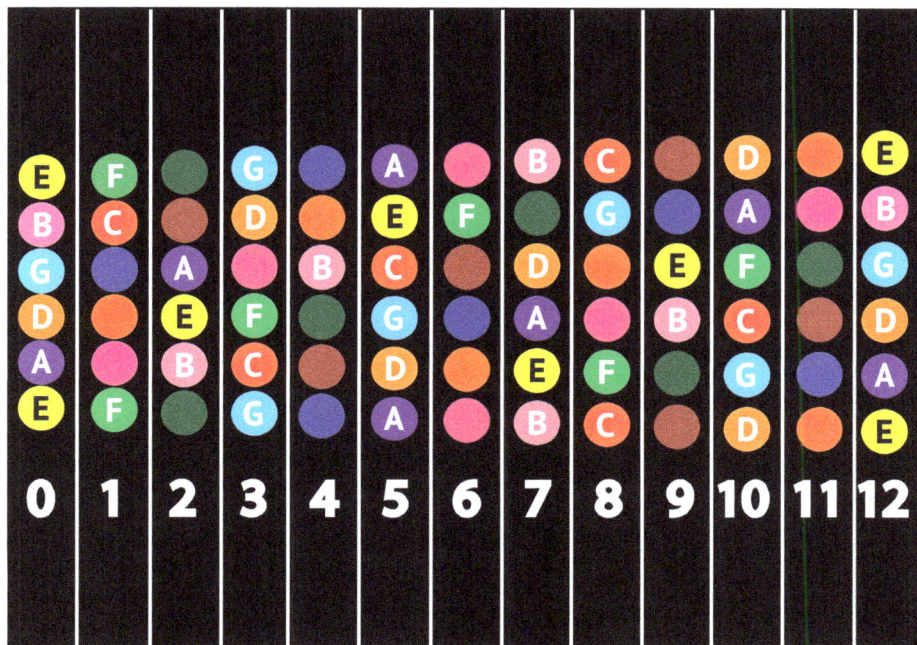

3/4 Size Acoustic (Age 8–12)

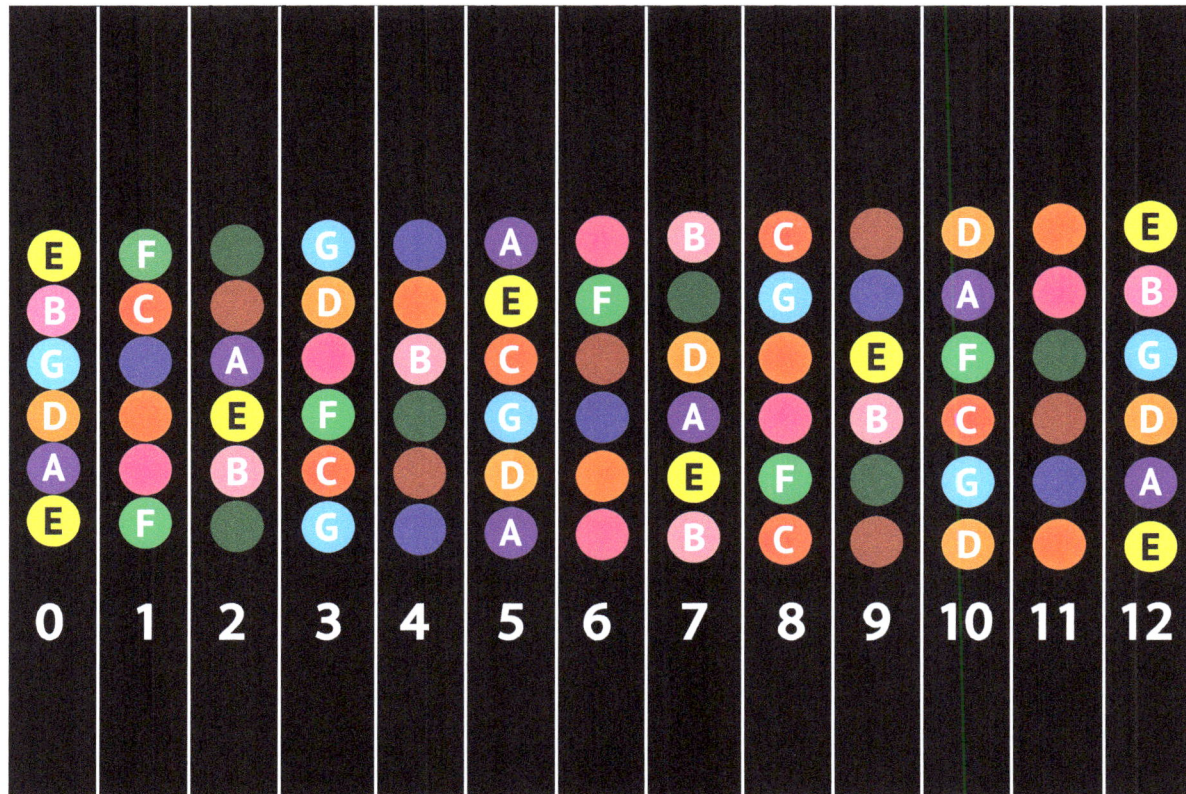

Full Size Wide-Neck Acoustic Guitar (Age 12+)

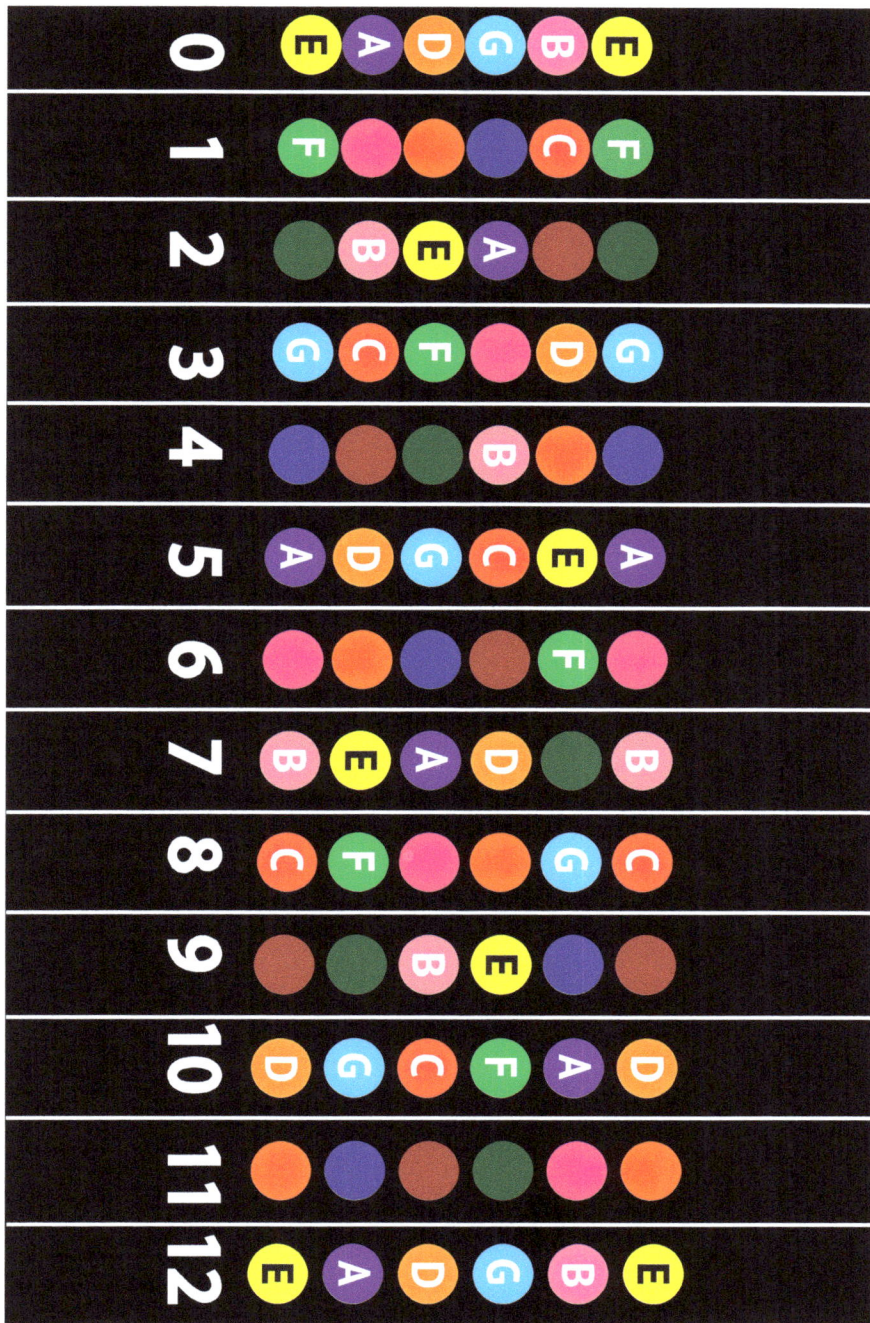

Congratulations!

(your name here)

worked hard
and completed

Play It!

LEVEL 1

Children's Songs
for Guitar

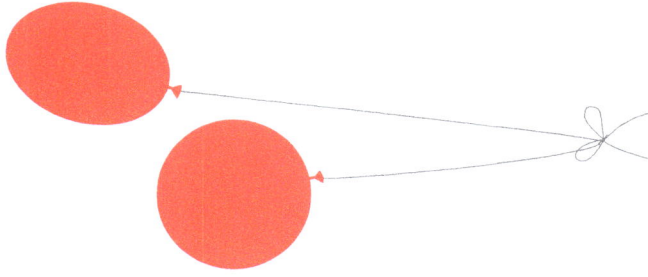

Make sure your
Play It!
library is complete

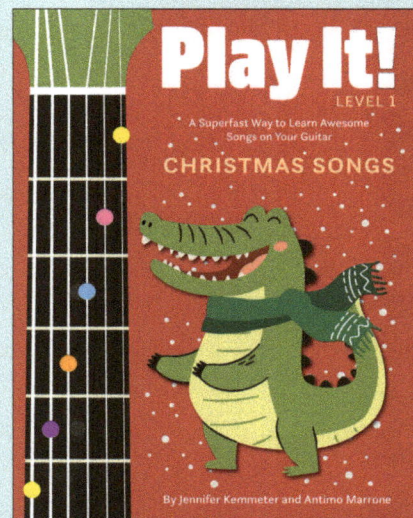

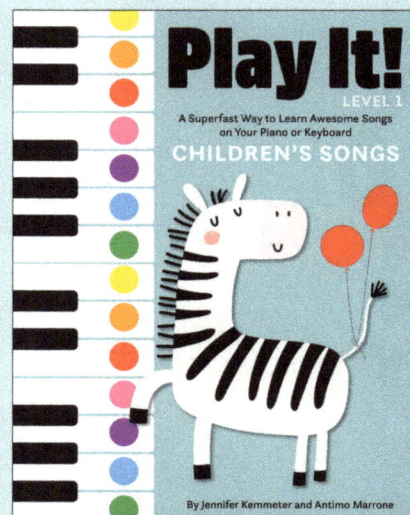

Play It! LEVEL 1
A Superfast Way to Learn Awesome Songs on Your Guitar
CHRISTMAS SONGS
By Jennifer Kemmeter and Antimo Marrone

Play It! LEVEL 1
A Superfast Way to Learn Awesome Songs on Your Piano or Keyboard
CHILDREN'S SONGS
By Jennifer Kemmeter and Antimo Marrone